Little Messages
from
God

and stories that
will warm your heart

giftables™

A division of Victory House, Inc.
Tulsa, Oklahoma

LITTLE MESSAGES FROM GOD
Copyright © 1999 by Victory House, Inc.
Cover design © 1999 by Victory House, Inc.
ISBN: 0-932081-68-1
Printed in the United States of America

Published by Victory House, Inc., P.O. Box 700238, Tulsa, Oklahoma 74170
(918) 747-5009

Cover design by: *Whitley Graphics*

Introduction

Filled with little messages from our great God, this special book is for everyone who is on a spiritual journey. The one-liners contain God's thoughts, and the heart-warming stories show how He is at work in people's lives today. Taken together, the messages and stories of this book will challenge, inspire, edify, and motivate you as they brighten your day in so many ways.

The uses of this book are as multitudinous as the messages themselves. First and foremost, it is a great giftbook for those you know and love. Its profound thoughts and vibrant humor are a great source of comfort and joy for those who are hospitalized or facing struggles of various kinds. The messages and stories provide fodder for public speakers, teachers, church bulletins, and pastors. People of all ages are moved when they ponder these personal messages from God's heart to theirs.

Little though they may be, the messages of this book are both thoughtful and thought-provoking. They give forth light and life to those who take time to listen and understand. Like a treasure chest filled with beautiful jewels, *Little Messages From God* is a valuable collection of glistening gems of wisdom, truth, and love. This truly unique book will embellish your life mentally, emotionally, and spiritually as you discover its insights and apply them to your life.

"Let's get together at My house this Sunday" (God).

"Have you read My Book lately? It will change your life" (God).

"It's time for us to talk things over" (God).

"*H*ave you prepared for your finals?" (God).

"*N*eed a counselor? I'm available" (God).

✧ ✧ ✧

"*I* said, 'Love your neighbor,' because that's the best way" (God).

"*I* love you just as you are" (God).

"*W*ent to see Dad. Be back to get you in a little while" (Jesus).

✧ ✧ ✧

"*W*here will the path you're on take you?" (God).

Jesus Loves Me

Karl Barth, a well-known theologian of the early twentieth century, wrote extensively about God and the Scriptures. On the occasion of his eightieth birthday a reporter asked, "Dr. Barth, what is the most important thing you have learned in all your years of studying about God and the Bible?" The German-Swiss intellectual paused a moment, then replied succinctly, "I think it is this — Jesus loves me, this I know, for the Bible tells me so."

"Jesus loves you" (God).

"*If* you were arrested for being a Christian would there be enough evidence to convict you?" (God).

✧ ✧ ✧

"*Why* don't you come over to My house and bring your wonderful kids?" (God).

"My children evolved from monkeys? You've gotta be kidding!" (God).

✧ ✧ ✧

"My way is always THE way" (God).

✧ ✧ ✧

"Every day tell your children that I love them" (God).

"You think it's hot in the summer?
I know a place that's a lot hotter"
(God).

✧ ✧ ✧

"When I said 'Thou shalt not. . . ,' I
meant *don't do it*" (God).

✧ ✧ ✧

"I'll always leave the Light on for
you" (God).

Life-Saving Prayer

During rush hour one morning a Christian lady came upon a scene that she will never forget. The traffic had come to a complete standstill, and as ambulances with wailing sirens came rushing by, she soon realized that a terrible accident had occurred. As she raised up in her seat she could see the tragic scene unfolding four or five car lengths ahead. While cars around her blared their horns in impatience this lady simply bowed her head in prayer. She asked God to minister to the person or persons who were injured.

Several months later, the lady learned what had happened. A stranger knocked at her door. She opened the door and invited her visitor inside. The person who had come to see her was a woman who was injured in the accident just described. The visitor said, "I've come to thank you for your prayer on the day of my accident five months ago. I nearly died, but I believe it was your prayer that saved me."

"I remember praying for whoever was hurt in the accident," the woman agreed, "but how did you know I had prayed?"

Her visitor responded, "As my spirit was leaving my body and was raised above the scene, everything was enshrouded by death and darkness. People were agitated and the negative energy and curses they were emitting had a serious effect upon my situation.

That was until you prayed. I remember looking at the row of cars in the traffic jam and my focus was directed to you. I saw you bow your head and pray. I even saw your license plate number. The minute you prayed, the clouds of gloom vanished and I was pulled back into my body."

She went on, "For several weeks I was in a coma, but when I awoke I had a vivid memory of you and your license number. I realized that your prayer had saved my life. I went to the Department of Transportation and they gave me your name and address. I just had to come to thank you. God bless you."

The two women wept, cried, and prayed together.

"Make prayer your first resort" (God).

"*I* love you and your spouse, and I'd like to be a part of your marriage" (God).

✧ ✧ ✧

"*L*et Me know what you need" (God).

✧ ✧ ✧

"*I*t's not smart to take My name in vain" (God).

"The benefits of the life insurance policy I offer are out of this world" (God).

✧ ✧ ✧

"You should see the mansion I've prepared for you" (Jesus).

✧ ✧ ✧

"If you're born twice you die only once" (God).

"*I* love to hear how much you love Me" (God).

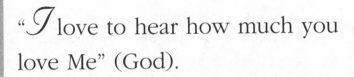

"*D*o you listen when I'm talking to you?" (God).

"*D*id you know that you're a King's kid?" (God).

Time

Imagine that there is a bank that credits your account each morning with $86,400. It carries over no balance from day to day. Every evening it deletes whatever part of the balance you failed to use during the day. What would you do? In all probability, you would withdraw every penny from your account each day.

Such a bank does exist. Its name is TIME. Every morning, it credits your account with 86,400 seconds. Every night it writes off, as lost, whatever amount of remaining time that you failed to invest to good purpose during the day. It carries over no balance,

20

and it permits no overdrafts. Each day a new account is opened in your name. If you fail to use the day's deposits, you experience a total loss of whatever time remains.

There is no going back, and there is no drawing against tomorrow. You must live in the present, on the day's deposits. That's why it's so important to invest the time you have each day so as to get the utmost return in the form of love, joy, peace, health, happiness, and success! The clock is running. Make the most of each day.

To realize the value of one year, ask a student who failed a grade or a prisoner who is confined for a year.

To realize the value of one month, ask a mother who gave birth to a premature infant.

To realize the value of one week, ask the editor of a weekly newspaper.

To realize the value of one hour, ask a student who is taking an hour-long final exam.

To realize the value of one minute, ask a person who just missed the train.

To realize the value of one second, ask a person who barely avoided an accident.

The most important letters in the English language are N-O-W. Treasure every moment you have! Time waits for no one. Yesterday is history. Tomorrow is a mystery. Today is a gift, and that's why it's called the present.

"Time is a precious gift. Use it wisely" (God).

"You must be born again" (Jesus).

✧ ✧ ✧

"You are very special to Me" (God).

✧ ✧ ✧

"Ten years from now, what will you wish you had done now?" (God).

Little Messages from God

"Follow Me" (Jesus).

"I want to be your Friend" (Jesus).

"Death is not a period — it is a comma in your life" (God).

"How soon you forget" (God).

25

"I know all your needs, and I want to meet each one" (God).

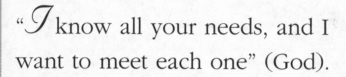

"Have no fear, I'm with you" (God).

"Contact Me to learn about a free trip to heaven" (God).

The Touch of the Master

Wishing to encourage her young son's progress on the piano, a mother took her boy to a Paderewski concert. After they were seated, the mother spotted a friend in the audience, and she walked down the aisle to greet her. While she was gone, the lad seized the opportunity to explore the great concert hall. Somehow he found his way through a door that was marked, "No Admittance."

When the house lights dimmed, the mother returned to her seat only to discover that her son was not there. She was seized with panic as the curtains parted and all eyes turned toward the impressive

Steinway on stage. In horror, the woman saw her son seated at the keyboard, and he was innocently picking out the bars of "Twinkle, Twinkle, Little Star."

Just then, the great piano master made his grand entrance. He quickly moved to the piano and whispered to the little boy, "Don't quit. Keep on playing." As he leaned over, Paderewski reached down with his left hand and began filling the bass part. Soon his right arm reached around to the other side of the child and the maestro added a running obbligato.

The old master transformed a potentially embarrassing, if not terrifying experience into a wonderfully creative experience for all concerned. The audience was delighted and mesmerized.

It is the same with our heavenly Father. The touch of the Master's hand makes all the difference. And sometimes when we face challenges and conflicts that seem to be too difficult, we hear the Master's voice whispering in our ear, "Don't quit. Keep playing." We feel His loving arms around us and our confidence is renewed.

"Don't quit. You and I can do it together" (God).

"*F*ight truth decay. Study your Bible daily" (God).

"*W*ork for Me. Though the work is hard and the hours are long, the retirement benefits are out of this world!" (God).

"*If* you're headed in the wrong direction I'll let you make a U-turn" (God).

✧ ✧ ✧

"*What* is missing in ch_ _ ch? UR" (God).

✧ ✧ ✧

"*My* power never fails" (God).

"*If* you don't like the way you were born, try being born again" (God).

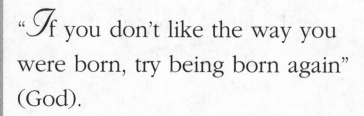

"*Don't* wait for the hearse to take you to church" (God).

The Wisdom of a Child

One Sunday in a Midwest city a young child was "acting up" during the morning worship hour. His parents did their best to maintain some semblance of order in the pew, but they were clearly losing the battle. Finally the father picked the little fellow up and walked sternly up the aisle on his way out. Just before reaching the safety of the foyer, the little boy called loudly to the congregation, "Please pray for me. Pray for me!"

"Prayer changes things" (God).

"I don't call only those who are equipped, but I do equip everyone I call" (God).

✧ ✧ ✧

"In the dark? Follow the Son" (God).

✧ ✧ ✧

"If you can't sleep, don't count sheep. Talk to the Shepherd" (God).

"I want your heart, even if it's broken" (God).

"Never, never, never give up" (God).

"The end of the story is better than the beginning" (God).

"When down in the mouth, remember Jonah — he came out all right" (God).

✧ ✧ ✧

"You can buy your education, but wisdom is a gift from Me" (God).

Be Careful What You Say

 woman had invited some people to dinner. At the table, she turned to her six-year-old daughter and asked, "Would you like to say the blessing?"

"I wouldn't know what to say," the little girl replied.

"Just say what you hear mommy say," the mother suggested.

"Okay," the girl began as they all bowed their heads, "Dear Lord, why on earth did I invite all these people to dinner?"

"Speak the truth in love" (God).

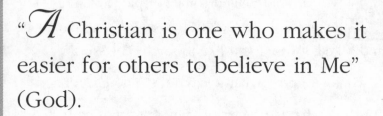

"*A* Christian is one who makes it easier for others to believe in Me" (God).

✧ ✧ ✧

"*D*on't fear tomorrow. I'm already there" (God).

"Though you don't know what the future holds, you can know the One who holds the future" (God).

"If I seem far away to you, who made the first move?" (God).

"*D*o what you can, and I'll do what you can't" (God).

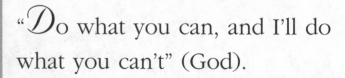

"*N*othing is impossible with God" (Jesus).

"*T*he word 'impossible' is not in My vocabulary" (God).

The Advantage of Faith

A Christian lady had to do a lot of traveling for her business, so she frequently found herself in airports and airplanes. Though flying made her nervous, she found that reading the Bible before, during, and after a flight would give her great peace.

A man sitting next to her on one of these flights noticed that she gave so much attention to the Bible and he chuckled sarcastically. He then challenged her with, "You don't really believe all that stuff in there, do you?"

"Of course I do. I believe every word of the Bible."

"Well, what about the guy who was supposedly swallowed by a whale? How can you believe that?" he queried.

"I believe it because it is in the Bible."

The man kept up his verbal assault. "How could anyone survive all that time inside a whale's stomach?"

"I don't have an answer to that question," the lady responded. "But when I get to heaven I'll ask Jonah about it."

"What if he isn't in heaven?" the man countered.

The woman replied, "Then *you* can ask him!"

"Eternity never ends" (God).

"If you keep Me outside, something must be wrong inside" (God).

✧ ✧ ✧

"When you're at the end of your rope it is there that you'll find Me" (God).

✧ ✧ ✧

"I am the Source" (God).

"*I* don't want My sheep to be sheepish" (God).

✧ ✧ ✧

"*W*hen I close one door I always open another" (God).

✧ ✧ ✧

"*N*othing will happen to you today that you and I can't handle together" (God).

"*T*he only thing I can't do is fail" (God).

"*T*wo people can't hate each other if they both love Me" (God).

"*S*ometimes trouble leads you to Me" (God).

Happiness Is a Journey

We convince ourselves that life will be better after we get married, have a baby, then another. Then we are frustrated that the kids aren't old enough and we'll be more content when they are. After that, we're frustrated that we have teenagers to deal with. We tell ourselves, "We will certainly be happy when they are out of that stage!"

We talk ourselves into believing that our lives will be complete when our spouse gets his/her act together, when we get a nicer car, when we graduate from college, when we get a promotion, when we are able to go on that long-dreamed-for vacation, or when we retire.

The truth is that there's no better time to be happy than right now. If not now, when? Your life will always be filled with challenges. So stop waiting until you finish school, go back to school, lose ten pounds, gain ten pounds, have kids, until your kids leave the house, until you start a new job, retire, get married, get divorced.

There's no better time than right now to be happy, because happiness is a journey, not a destination.

"Happiness comes from within" (God).

"It's harder not to believe in Me than it is to believe in Me" (God).

✧ ✧ ✧

"I have two dwelling places: heaven and a thankful heart" (God).

✧ ✧ ✧

"It's hard to hate someone you're praying for" (God).

"*I* am a present help in trouble, and I am a great help for keeping you out of trouble" (God).

"*I*'ve invited you to My house. When will you invite Me to your house?" (God).

"*Y*ou've tried everything else. Why not try Me?" (God).

✧ ✧ ✧

"*A* lot of kneeling keeps you standing" (God).

✧ ✧ ✧

"*M*y commandments permit no amendments" (God).

Thoughts for the Day

Work like you don't need the money.

Love like you've never been hurt.

Live like you're not afraid to die.

Play like a child.

And laugh like no one's listening.

"Choose life" (God).

"There are two kinds of folks in hell — those who will do anything and those who won't do anything!" (God).

"Do unto others as if you were the others" (God).

"*I* really do care" (God).

"*H*ell is not air-conditioned"
(God).

✧ ✧ ✧

"*H*ell may seem out of date to
you, but it's not out of business"
(God).

"The church is full of hypocrites, and there's always room for one more" (God).

"Christians aren't perfect, but they are forgiven" (God).

"No loaves to a loafer" (God).

The Power of Choice

Bill is a perennial optimist. He always seems to be in a good mood, and he always has something positive to say. When someone asked him how he was doing, he would always reply, "If I were any better, I'd be twins!"

As the manager of a restaurant Bill influenced many people, including customers and staff. As a matter of fact, several waiters followed him from restaurant to restaurant whenever he relocated. They found Bill's attitude to be attractive, and this made him a natural motivator. When an employee was having a bad day, Bill would help the worker find the positive side of the situation.

One day an employee went up to Bill and said, "I don't get it! How can you be such a positive person all the time?"

Bill's answer was a simple one: "Each morning I wake up and say to myself, 'Bill, you have two choices today. You can choose to be in a good mood, or you can choose to be in a bad mood. I always choose to be in a good mood. Then, every time something bad happens, I can choose to be a victim, or I can choose to learn something from it. I always try to choose to learn from the situation. The same thing is true whenever someone comes to me with a complaint. I can either choose to accept their complaining, or I can point them in a more positive direction. I always try to choose the latter."

"I'm sorry," the employee interjected. "It can't possibly be that easy!"

'Yes, it is," Bill replied. "Life is all about choices. When you cut away all the junk, you soon see that every situation is a choice. It is our responsibility to choose how we will react to the circumstances and how others will affect your mood. Whether you are in a good mood or a bad mood is your choice. The bottom line is that it's simply your choice how you approach life and the circumstances of your life."

The employee thought about Bill's words over and over again after he left his employ. Several years later the worker heard that Bill had done something that a manager of a restaurant should never do — he left the back door open as he was counting the day's receipts after closing. Three robbers came in and held him at gunpoint. While Bill struggled to open the safe, his hand slipped off the dial. The robbers panicked and shot him several times.

After eighteen hours of surgery and weeks of intensive care, Bill was released from the hospital, but he still had fragments of the bullets in his body. Bill's former employee went to the man who had left such an impression on him. "How're you doing, Bill?" the young man asked.

"If I were doing any better, I'd be twins," he laughed. "Wanna see my scars?"

"No, thanks, but I was wondering what went through your mind as the robbery was taking place," the former employee asked.

Bill's answer seemed familiar. "The first thing that went through my mind was the thought that I should have locked the door. Then, while I was lying on the floor, I remembered that I had two choices. I could either choose to live or I could choose to die."

The friend asked, "Weren't you scared? Didn't you lose consciousness?"

Bill went on, "The paramedics were great. They kept telling me I would be fine. But when they wheeled me into the ER and I saw the expressions on the faces of the doctors and nurses, I did get scared. I could read their eyes which seemed to be saying, 'He's a dead man!' It was then that I knew I needed to take positive action."

"What did you do?"

"A nurse began shouting questions at me. She asked if I was allergic to anything. I said, 'Yes,' then I took a deep breath and said, 'bullets!' Over the laughter of the medical team, I announced, "I am choosing to live. So please operate on me as if I'm alive, not dead!"

Bill chose to live, and that's exactly what happened. He recovered. He's a restaurant manager again, and he continues to sow seeds of happiness and gratitude wherever he goes.

"Your attitude is half the battle" (God).

"Never judge another by his relatives because he did not choose them" (God).

"Praying is like eating peanuts. The more you do it, the more you want to do it" (God).

"*A*n atheist has nobody to talk to when he is alone" (God).

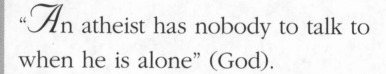

"*F*amilies that pray together stay together" (God).

"*L*ove Me with all your heart" (God).

"*L*ife is fragile — handle with prayer" (God).

❖ ❖ ❖

"*I*f you are too busy to pray, you're too busy" (God).

❖ ❖ ❖

"*T*he secret of prayer is prayer in secret" (God).

Still My Friend

As you got up this morning, I watched you and hoped you would talk to me, even if it were just a few words, asking my opinion or thanking me for something good that happened in your life yesterday, but I noticed you were too busy trying to find the right outfit to put on and wear to work.

I waited again. When you ran around the house getting ready, I knew there would be a few minutes for you to stop and say hello, but you were too busy. At one point you had to wait fifteen minutes with nothing to do except sit in a chair. Then I saw you spring to your feet. I thought you wanted to talk to me, but you ran to the phone and called a friend to get the latest gossip.

I watched as you went to work, and I waited patiently all day long. With all your activities, I guess you were too busy to say anything to me. I noticed that before lunch you looked around. Maybe you felt embarrassed to talk to me, that is why you didn't bow your head. You glanced three or four tables over and you noticed some of your friends talking to me briefly before they ate, but you didn't. That's okay. There is still more time left, and I have hope that you will talk to me even yet.

You went home, and it seems as if you had lots of things to do. After a few of them were done, you turned on the TV. I don't know if I like TV or not, just about anything goes there and you spend a lot of time each day in front of it — not thinking about anything — just enjoying the show.

I waited patiently again as you watched TV and ate your meal, but again you didn't talk to me. As you did your paperwork I waited again. You did what you had to do. At bedtime I guess you felt too tired. After you said good night to your family, you plopped into bed and fell asleep in no time. That's okay, because you may not realize that I am always there for you.

I've got more patience than you will ever know. I even want to teach you how to be patient with others as well. Because I love you so much, a long time ago

I left a wonderful place called heaven, and came to earth. I gave it up so that I could be ridiculed and made fun of. And I even died so that I could take your place. I love you so much that I wait every day for a nod, prayers, thought, or thanksgiving.

It is hard to have a one-sided conversation. Well, I see you are getting up again and once more I will wait with nothing but love for you, hoping that today you will give me some time. Have a nice day!

Your friend, Jesus.

"What a Friend you have in Jesus" (God).

"The family altar will alter your family" (God).

✧ ✧ ✧

"About the only thing that comes to people who procrastinate is old age" (God).

✧ ✧ ✧

"What have you done for others today?" (God).

"A really good golfer is one who goes to church on Sunday first" (God).

✧ ✧ ✧

"The best attitude is gratitude" (God).

✧ ✧ ✧

"How long do you plan to keep on doing that?" (God).

"It is more blessed to give than to receive" (God).

"Fear of the future is a waste of the present" (God).

"Feed your faith and your doubts will starve to death" (God).

A Child's Insights

A little boy offered his prayers one night and his parents overheard him say, "Dear God, please take care of mom and dad and look after my sisters and brothers and me. And please, God, take good care of yourself. If anything should happen to you, we are all sunk."

"I am proud to be your Father" (God).

"*A* faith lift will do more for you than a face lift will" (God).

✧ ✧ ✧

"*D*on't grab the steering wheel after you ask Me to guide your life" (God).

✧ ✧ ✧

"*W*ho said, 'Nobody will know'?" (God).

"I see everything you do" (God).

"The best way out is always through" (God).

"Failure is not the worst thing in the world. The worst thing is not to try" (God).

"There are no detours on heaven's road" (God).

✧ ✧ ✧

"The most desirable time to read your Bible is as often as possible" (God).

✧ ✧ ✧

"The best things in life are not things" (God).

An Octogenarian's Humor

When Winston Churchill turned eighty-two a young photographer was assigned to take his picture. The photographer looked at the former prime minister and said, "I hope I may have the privilege of taking your picture again when you are 100."

Sir Winston replied, "No reason why you shouldn't — if you continue to look after your health."

"A merry heart is as good as a medicine" (God).

"Only you can damage your character" (God).

✧ ✧ ✧

"If you died tonight, where would you spend eternity?" (God).

✧ ✧ ✧

"You're important to Me. What's most important to you?" (God).

"Who's number one in your life?"
(God).

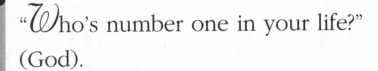

"It's what you are, not where you
are that determines your happiness"
(God).

"Where will you spend eternity?
Smoking, or non-smoking?" (God).

"*P*rofanity is evidence of a weak vocabulary and a weak brain" (God).

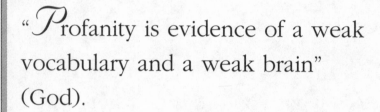

"*G*et ready for eternity. You're going to spend a lot of time there" (God).

The Most Remarkable Salesman in the World

Christopher Columbus was quite a salesman. He started out by not knowing where he was going. When he got there, he didn't know where he was. When he returned, he didn't know where he had been. He did all this on borrowed money, and even so, he managed to get a repeat order!

"Keep on keeping on" (God).

"*I*f you marry a child of the devil you can expect to have trouble with your father-in-law" (God).

"*T*he greatest riches are things that money can't buy" (God).

"*O*nly what you give away do you get to keep for all eternity" (God).

"*H*ot heads and cold hearts resolve nothing, but cool heads and warm hearts resolve much" (God).

"*I*n the light of eternity what's really important?" (God).

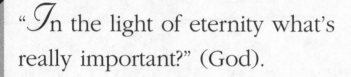

"*M*oney can build a house, but it takes love to build a home" (God).

"*O*pen up your heart and let My Son shine in" (God).

Time and Money

A man prayed, "Lord, is it true that a day is like a thousand years to you, and a penny is like a thousand dollars?"

The Lord answered, "Yes."

"Well," the man responded, "then can I have a penny?"

The Lord answered, "In a day or two."

"Make the most of what you have" (God).

"Your life has a purpose. Have you discovered what it is?" (God).

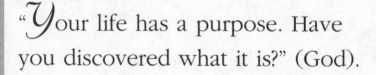

"The truth will set you free" (Jesus).

"Who said, 'There is no God'?" (God).

"Who said, 'God is not fair'?"
(God).

"I've never wondered if *you* exist"
(God).

"Who said, 'God doesn't hear me
when I pray'?" (God).

"Who said, 'Heaven is a pipe-dream'?" (God).

✧ ✧ ✧

"I hear every word you speak" (God).

✧ ✧ ✧

"Who said, 'God has forgotten all about me'?" (God).

George Washington Carver

As a young man on a peanut plantation down south George Washington Carver was contemplating his future. He looked up at heaven and asked, "Lord, do you want me to discover why you created the universe?"

The Lord replied, "No, that's too big for you."

"Well, do you want me to discover why you created the earth?"

The Lord replied, "No, that's too big for you."

Just then, the young man stumbled over a hill of peanuts. He reached down and picked up a peanut.

Then he asked, "Do you want me to discover why you created the peanut?"

The Lord replied, "That's just your size!"

George Washington Carver went on to discover over 100 uses for the lowly peanut, including the wonderful food we call peanut butter.

"I have a plan and a purpose for your life" (God).

"Who said, 'I'll never forgive you'?" (God).

"Who said, 'My Word contradicts itself'?" (God).

✧ ✧ ✧

"There are no short-cuts on the way to heaven" (God).

"*W*ho said, 'Life isn't worth living'?" (God).

✧ ✧ ✧

"*I*t is appointed unto man once to die, and then the judgment" (God).

✧ ✧ ✧

"*W*hy are you afraid of death?" (God).

"*I* live in heaven, but I want to live in your heart" (God).

"*If* you want to see circumstances and other people change you must first change yourself" (God).

"*Who* made you?" (God).

It's Never Too Late!

A remarkable woman named Helen received her high school diploma when she was ninety-three years old. Finally receiving her diploma filled her with joy. She had actually graduated in 1907, but the school was so much in debt that it could not afford to have diplomas printed. She could not share her excitement with her fellow-classmates, unfortunately, because she was the only surviving member of her class. Nonetheless, yesterday's disappointment had been transformed into sheer joy — a reminder to all of us that it's never too late.

"My timing is perfect" (God).

"If you want to become great choose to become the servant of all" (Jesus).

✧ ✧ ✧

"Three things that you can give away and still keep are a smile, your word, and a grateful heart" (God).

"*B*e yourself. Nobody else can be as good as you at being you" (God).

✧ ✧ ✧

"*M*y rules have never changed" (God).

✧ ✧ ✧

"*W*ise men still seek Me" (Jesus).

"Of course I still love you. I'm your Father" (God).

✧ ✧ ✧

"I am not finished with you yet" (God).

✧ ✧ ✧

"You may think you're finished with Me, but I'm not finished with you" (God).

Something to Remember

Some time ago, a father who was undergoing some financial distress prior to the Christmas holidays punished his three-year-old daughter for wasting a roll of gold wrapping paper. Money was tight that year, and he became infuriated when the child tried to decorate a box to put under the tree. Nevertheless, the little girl brought the gift to her father the next morning and said, "This is for you, daddy."

He was embarrassed by his earlier overreaction, but his anger flared again when he found that the box was empty. He then yelled at his daughter, "Don't you know that when you give someone a present, there's supposed to be something inside of it?"

The little girl looked up at him with tears in her eyes and said, "Oh, daddy, it's not empty. I blew kisses into the box. All for you, daddy."

The father was crushed. He put his arms around his little girl, and he begged her forgiveness. From that time on he cherished the little gold box which he kept by his bed for many years. Whenever he was discouraged, he would take out an imaginary kiss and remember the love of the child who had put it there. In a very real sense, each of us has been given a gold container filled with unconditional love and kisses.

There is no more precious possession anyone could hold.

"Do you know how much I love you?" (God).

"Just who do you think you are, and who do you think I am?" (God).

✦ ✦ ✦

"Be careful, or I might have to leave you alone" (God).

✦ ✦ ✦

"I'm working hard in your behalf. Won't you join Me?" (God).

"Did you hug your kids today?"
(God).

✧ ✧ ✧

"Did you hug your spouse today?"
(God).

✧ ✧ ✧

"The things that count most in life
are the things that can't be counted"
(God).

"Remember Me?" (God).

"You can't change My mind, but I can help you change yours" (God).

"Did you take time to appreciate the flowers I gave you today?" (God).

A Father's Love

A father's college-age daughter was brutally raped and murdered. The young man who committed this heinous crime was caught, convicted, and incarcerated. He ended up on death row.

The young lady's father was emotionally torn. Hate and anger flooded his being. His pastor told him to go to prayer until he found peace. He tried and tried, but every attempt at prayer was like a wrestling match.

He kept trying to reach God. One night, as he was on the verge of sleep, he prayed earnestly. Light filled his room and the voice of God came through loudly and clearly. The man heard only one word from the voice of God: "Forgive."

Almost defiantly, the man shouted, "How can I forgive the man who murdered my daughter? I loved her so much."

"It's a choice you must make."

Now the father knew that he had no alternative. He accepted what God had told him, and through sheer determination of his will, he chose to forgive his daughter's murderer. This was a decision, not a feeling, but the more he committed himself to it, he discovered that some of the feelings of hatred, fear, contempt, and depression began to lift.

Deep within, he knew he could not stop here. He knew he had to do more. "I will go to the man on death row in order to let him know that I forgive him."

The next weekend that's exactly what the father did. The convict greeted him with reservation and trepidation as the father of the woman he murdered shared his heart with him. He listened intently as the man told him what he had gone through as a result of what the young man had done.

A reporter from the local newspaper was on hand. He, too, was moved by the father's story, especially the attitude that he conveyed. That same morning the father of the murdered co-ed was privileged to be able to lead his daughter's murderer to Jesus Christ.

It was a divine encounter. The father chose to overcome evil with good. The two men embraced.

The next Sunday, the newspaper reporter wrote, "I think I've just met my first Christian."

"Overcome evil with good" (God).

"*H*ave you forgotten what you promised?" (God).

✧ ✧ ✧

"*F*orgiveness is a choice" (God).

✧ ✧ ✧

"*A*re you afraid of the dark? Let Me give you light" (God).

"*I* love you, but I hate your sin" (God).

"*T*ake My hand, and I'll lift you up" (God).

"*I*t's always nice to hear from you" (God).

"*Forgive*" (God).

✧ ✧ ✧

"*Love* is a commitment" (God).

✧ ✧ ✧

"*One* reason why you should love your enemies is because without them you'd have nobody to blame but yourself" (God).

Under His Wings

An article in *National Geographic* several years ago provides us with a penetrating look at God's love and care. After a forest fire in Yellowstone National Park, forest rangers began their trek up a mountain in order to assess the damage that had been done.

One ranger found a bird that was literally petrified in ashes, but perched like a statue on the ground at the base of a badly scorched tree. Somewhat sickened by the eerie sight, the park ranger knocked the bird over with a stick.

As he struck the bird, three tiny chicks scurried out from under the wings of their dead mother. The loving mother, keenly aware of the impending disaster, had carried her offspring to the base of the tree and had gathered them under her wings, somehow instinctively knowing that the smoke could asphyxiate them.

She could have flown to safety, but had refused to abandon her babies. When the blaze had arrived, and the heat had scorched her small body, the mother had remained steadfast. Because she had been willing to die, those under the cover of her wings continued to live.

God, like the mother bird, is always there to protect us. The Bible says, "He will cover you with his feathers, and under his wings you will find refuge" (Ps. 91:4).

"Trust Me" (God).

"*P*lease take care of yourself" (God).

✧ ✧ ✧

"*I*'m still waiting, but I won't wait forever" (God).

✧ ✧ ✧

"*M*ake your purpose in life to see others through, not to see through others" (God).

"Careful what you say. It may be used against you" (God).

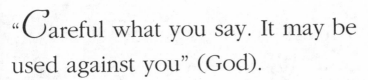

"I created you in My image" (God).

"Want to make Me laugh? Tell Me what *you* have planned" (God).

"Sin will take you further than you want to go, keep you longer than you want to stay and cost you more than you want to pay" (God).

✧ ✧ ✧

"Be like a turtle. The only time it makes progress is when it sticks its neck out" (God).

A Vision of Jesus

A little girl who was sick in bed noticed a mirror on the wall across from the foot of her bed. In the mirror she could see the picture of Jesus that hung above the head of her bed.

As she started to feel a little better, she would rise up in her bed and look into the mirror. She saw herself, and she began to cry.

Her mother heard her whimpering and rushed to her aid. "What's wrong, honey?"

"Mommy, I just realized that every time I see myself I can't see Jesus!"

"Turn your eyes upon Jesus" (God).

"Have you counted all the gifts I gave you today?" (God).

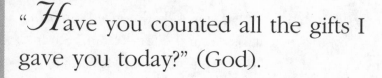

"Please do something for Me" (God).

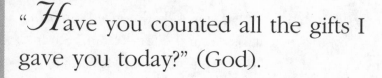

"Give, give, give, give" (God).

"Someday you'll have to tell Me why you did that" (God).

✧ ✧ ✧

"Why do you always wait until the last minute to talk to Me?" (God).

✧ ✧ ✧

"Why do you blame Me when everything goes wrong?" (God).

"To be truly successful in life, give and forgive" (God)."

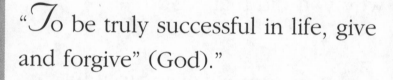

"Someday you'll have to tell Me why you said that" (God).

The Most Caring Child

Leo Buscaglia once talked about a contest he was asked to judge. The purpose of the contest was to find the most caring child.

The winner was a four-year-old child whose next-door neighbor was an elderly gentleman who had just lost his wife. When the little boy saw the man cry, he went over into the man's yard, climbed onto his lap, and just sat there.

His mother saw what had taken place. When her son returned she asked, "What did you say to Mr. Boynton?"

"Nothing. I just helped him cry."

"Keep a tender heart" (God).

"I'm your mighty buckler, but not your mighty butler" (God).

✧ ✧ ✧

"I've given you both time and talent. If you use your time well, you may even surpass those of greater ability" (God).

✧ ✧ ✧

"You're welcome" (God).

"*D*id you forget to thank Me today?" (God).

"*S*ee, you really do need Me" (God).

"*W*hen I invited two snails on board the ark they showed us the value of persistence" (God).

What It Means to Be Adopted

A first-grade teacher's pupils were discussing a picture of a family. One little boy in the picture had hair that was different in color than every other member of the family. One child suggested that he was adopted. Another little girl remarked, "I know all about adoptions, because I was adopted."

Another child asked, "What does it mean to be adopted?"

"It means," the adopted girl explained, "that I grew in my mommy's heart instead of her tummy."

"I have chosen you" (God).

"*D*on't blame Me for the messes you create" (God).

✧ ✧ ✧

"*K*eep your eyes on the prize" (God).

✧ ✧ ✧

"*T*he only way to the mountaintop is through the valley" (God).

"Everyone's day is twenty-four hours long, so no one has the advantage" (God).

✧ ✧ ✧

"A truly humble person doesn't think less of himself; he just thinks about himself less" (God).

✧ ✧ ✧

"Am I everything to you?" (God).

Barney

A four-year-old went with her mother for a check-up at the pediatrician's. As the doctor examined her ears with an otoscope, he asked, "Do you think I'll find Big Bird in here?" The little girl remained silent.

Next, the doctor took a tongue depressor and looked down her throat. He asked, "Do you think I'll find the Cookie Monster down there?"

Again, the little girl maintained her silence. Then the doctor put a stethoscope on her chest. As he listened to her heart beat, he asked, "Do you think I'll hear Barney in there?"

Finally, the little girl responded. "Oh, no," she countered, "Jesus is in my heart, but Barney's on my underwear."

"Unless you become like a little child. . ." (Jesus).

"Between yesterday and tomorrow is the most important time of all" (God).

✧ ✧ ✧

"Circumstances are not your lord, and emotions are not your master" (God).

✧ ✧ ✧

"You get what you expect" (God).

"Before you can lead others you must get control of yourself" (God).

✧ ✧ ✧

"Experience is a hard teacher because it gives the test first and the lesson afterward" (God).

✧ ✧ ✧

"Loving contains its own reward" (God).

Discouraged?

As I was driving home from work one day, I stopped to watch a Little League game that was being played in a ballpark near my home.

As I sat down on a bench behind the first-base line, I asked one of the boys what the score was. "We're behind 14 to nothing," he answered with a sheepish smile.

"Really?" I replied. "I have to say you don't look very discouraged."

"Discouraged?" the boy asked with a puzzled look on his face. "Why should we be discouraged? We haven't been up to bat yet!"

"Never, never lose hope" (God).

"*I*t's your attitude, not your aptitude, that determines your altitude" (God).

✧ ✧ ✧

"*I*t's the dream that makes the person" (God).

✧ ✧ ✧

"*Y*ou and Me together are a majority" (God).

"*I* have no grandchildren" (God).

"*F*orbidden fruit creates many jams" (God).

"*W*hat goes around comes around" (God).

All the World's a Stage

Whenever I'm disappointed with my spot in my life, I stop and think about little Johnny Smith. Johnny was trying out for a part in a school play. His mother told me that he's set his heart on being in it, though she feared he would not be chosen to perform.

On the day when the parts were awarded, I went with her to pick him up after school. Johnny rushed up to her, his eyes shining with pride and excitement.

"Guess what, mom?" he shouted, and then said the following words which will always be a lesson to me. "I've been chosen to clap and cheer!" he beamed.

"Make the best of every situation" (God).

"I will never leave you" (God).

"Let Me help you carry your burdens" (God).

"I am speaking. Are you listening?" (God).

"Draw near to Me, and I will draw near to you" (God).

✧ ✧ ✧

"I'm only a prayer away" (God).

✧ ✧ ✧

"I am love" (God).

✧ ✧ ✧

"I'm watching out for you" (God).

A Lesson in Heart

Susan was born with a muscle missing in her foot. Her condition requires her to wear a brace at all times. Though this would seem challenging to many ten-year-olds, it was not so with Susan. She came home from school on a beautiful spring day to announce that she had competed in the field day program.

I began to wonder what I might say to encourage her, because I knew how difficult it must have been for her to compete with the others, but my thoughts were interrupted by her joyous tones, "Daddy, I won two of the races!"

Neither her dad nor I could believe what she was saying.

Susan explained, "I had an advantage."

I reasoned that she must have been given a head start or something.

As if she could read my mind, the little girl went on to say, "Daddy, I didn't get a head start. My advantage was that I had to try harder!"

"Keep on trying" (God).

"I'm never asleep" (God).

"There is one way to stay out of hell, but no way to get out" (God).

"If you give something to Me, don't take it back" (God).

"Satan has an excuse for every sin" (God).

✧ ✧ ✧

"Owning a Bible is a tremendous responsibility" (God).

✧ ✧ ✧

"You can't hide from Me" (God).

If Only I Could Become
One of Them

It was a cold, blustery day and the farmer was about to turn the lights out in his garage when he noticed that a little bird had gotten trapped inside. The frightened creature was flying about aimlessly, trying desperately to find a way out of the building. In the process, the bird flew hard against the garage window several times. It would fall to the floor each time, quite dazed, and the farmer would try to pick it up, but each time he did so, the startled bird managed to fly well above his reach.

He did everything he knew to do to get the bird to fly out the open garage door, but the raging winds prevented this from happening. The farmer scratched his head in frustration as he began to think. "If only I could become a bird, I could lead her safely out."

This is how God has responded to us. He sent His Son to become one of us so He could lead us to safety. All we have to do is follow Him.

"Follow Jesus" (God).